Francis Frith's
AROUND SOUTHAMPTON

PHOTOGRAPHIC MEMORIES

Francis Frith's
AROUND SOUTHAMPTON

◆

Nick Channer

FRITH
BOOK Co

First published in the United Kingdom in 2000 by
Frith Book Company Ltd

Hardback Edition 2000
ISBN 1-85937-088-8

Paperback Edition 2001
ISBN 1-85937-427-1

British Library Cataloguing in Publication Data

Francis Frith's Around Southampton
Nick Channer

Frith Book Company Ltd
Frith's Barn, Teffont,
Salisbury, Wiltshire SP3 5QP
Tel: +44 (0) 1722 716 376
Email: info@frithbook.co.uk
www.frithbook.co.uk

Printed and bound in Great Britain

CONTENTS

FRANCIS FRITH: *Victorian Pioneer*

FRANCIS FRITH, Victorian founder of the world-famous photographic archive, was a complex and multitudinous man. A devout Quaker and a highly successful Victorian businessman, he was both philosophic by nature and pioneering in outlook.

By 1855 Francis Frith had already established a wholesale grocery business in Liverpool, and sold it for the astonishing sum of £200,000, which is the equivalent today of over £15,000,000. Now a multi-millionaire, he was able to indulge his passion for travel. As a child he had pored over travel books written by early explorers, and his fancy and imagination had been stirred by family holidays to the sublime mountain regions of Wales and Scotland. 'What a land of spirit-stirring and enriching scenes and places!' he had written. He was to return to these scenes of grandeur in later years to 'recapture the thousands of vivid and tender memories', but with a different purpose. Now in his thirties, and captivated by the new science of photography, Frith set out on a series of pioneering journeys to the Nile regions that occupied him from 1856 until 1860.

INTRIGUE AND ADVENTURE

He took with him on his travels a specially-designed wicker carriage that acted as both dark-room and sleeping chamber. These far-flung journeys were packed with intrigue and adventure. In his life story, written when he was sixty-three, Frith tells of being held captive by bandits, and of fighting 'an awful midnight battle to the very point of surrender with a deadly pack of hungry, wild dogs'. Sporting flowing Arab costume, Frith arrived at Akaba by camel seventy years before Lawrence, where he encountered 'desert princes and rival sheikhs, blazing with jewel-hilted swords'.

During these extraordinary adventures he was assiduously exploring the desert regions bordering the Nile and patiently recording the antiquities and peoples with his camera. He was the first photographer to venture beyond the sixth cataract. Africa was still the mysterious 'Dark Continent', and Stanley and Livingstone's historic meeting was a decade into the future. The conditions for picture taking confound belief. He laboured for hours in his wicker dark-room in the sweltering heat of the desert, while the volatile chemicals fizzed dangerously in their trays. Often he was forced to work in remote tombs and caves where conditions were cooler. Back in London he exhibited his photographs and was 'rapturously cheered' by members of the Royal Society. His reputation as a photographer was made overnight. An eminent modern historian has likened their impact on the population of the time to that on our own generation of the first photographs taken on the surface of the moon.

VENTURE OF A LIFE-TIME

Characteristically, Frith quickly spotted the opportunity to create a new business as a specialist publisher of photographs. He lived in an era of immense and sometimes violent change. For the poor in the early part of Victoria's reign work was a drudge and the hours long, and people had precious little free time to enjoy themselves.

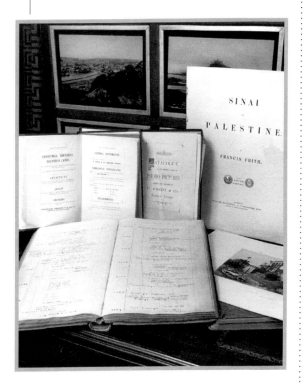

Most had no transport other than a cart or gig at their disposal, and had not travelled far beyond the boundaries of their own town or village. However, by the 1870s, the railways had threaded their way across the country, and Bank Holidays and half-day Saturdays had been made obligatory by Act of Parliament. All of a sudden the ordinary working man and his family were able to enjoy days out and see a little more of the world.

With characteristic business acumen, Francis Frith foresaw that these new tourists would enjoy having souvenirs to commemorate their days out. In 1860 he married Mary Ann Rosling and set out with the intention of photographing every city, town and village in Britain. For the next thirty years he travelled the country by train and by pony and trap, producing fine photographs of seaside resorts and beauty spots that were keenly bought by millions of Victorians. These prints were painstakingly pasted into family albums and pored over during the dark nights of winter, rekindling precious memories of summer excursions.

THE RISE OF FRITH & CO

Frith's studio was soon supplying retail shops all over the country. To meet the demand he gathered about him a small team of photographers, and published the work of independent artist-photographers of the calibre of Roger Fenton and Francis Bedford. In order to gain some understanding of the scale of Frith's business one only has to look at the catalogue issued by Frith & Co in 1886: it runs to some 670

pages, listing not only many thousands of views of the British Isles but also many photographs of most European countries, and China, Japan, the USA and Canada – note the sample page shown above from the hand-written *Frith & Co* ledgers detailing pictures taken. By 1890 Frith had created the greatest specialist photographic publishing company in the world, with over 2,000 outlets – more than the combined number that Boots and WH Smith have today! The picture on the right shows the *Frith & Co* display board at Ingleton in the Yorkshire Dales. Beautifully constructed with mahogany frame and gilt inserts, it could display up to a dozen local scenes.

POSTCARD BONANZA

◆

The ever-popular holiday postcard we know today took many years to develop. In 1870 the Post Office issued the first plain cards, with a pre-printed stamp on one face. In 1894 they allowed other publishers' cards to be sent through the mail with an attached adhesive halfpenny stamp. Demand grew rapidly, and in 1895 a new size of postcard was permitted called the

court card, but there was little room for illustration. In 1899, a year after Frith's death, a new card measuring 5.5 x 3.5 inches became the standard format, but it was not until 1902 that the divided back came into being, with address and message on one face and a full-size illustration on the other. *Frith & Co* were in the vanguard of postcard development, and Frith's sons Eustace and Cyril continued their father's monumental task, expanding the number of views offered to the public and recording more and more places in Britain, as the coasts and countryside were opened up to mass travel.

Francis Frith died in 1898 at his villa in Cannes, his great project still growing. The archive he created continued in business for another seventy years. By 1970 it contained over a third of a million pictures of 7,000 cities, towns and villages. The massive photographic record Frith has left to us stands as a living monument to a special and very remarkable man.

Frith's Archive: *A Unique Legacy*

FRANCIS FRITH'S legacy to us today is of immense significance and value, for the magnificent archive of evocative photographs he created provides a unique record of change in 7,000 cities, towns and villages throughout Britain over a century and more. Frith and his fellow studio photographers revisited locations many times down the years to update their views, compiling for us an enthralling and colourful pageant of British life and character.

We tend to think of Frith's sepia views of Britain as nostalgic, for most of us use them to conjure up memories of places in our own lives with which we have family associations. It often makes us forget that to Francis Frith they were records of daily life as it was actually being lived in the cities, towns and villages of his day. The Victorian

age was one of great and often bewildering change for ordinary people, and though the pictures evoke an impression of slower times, life was as busy and hectic as it is today.

We are fortunate that Frith was a photographer of the people, dedicated to recording the minutiae of everyday life. For it is this sheer wealth of visual data, the painstaking chronicle of changes in dress, transport, street layouts, buildings, housing, engineering and landscape that captivates us so much today. His remarkable images offer us a powerful link with the past and with the lives of our ancestors.

TODAY'S TECHNOLOGY

Computers have now made it possible for Frith's many thousands of images to be accessed almost instantly. In the Frith archive today, each photograph is carefully 'digitised' then stored on a CD Rom. Frith archivists can locate a single photograph amongst thousands within seconds. Views can be catalogued and sorted under a variety of categories of place and content to the immediate benefit of researchers. Inexpensive reference prints can be created for them at the touch of a mouse button, and a wide range of books and other printed materials assembled and published for a wider, more general readership - in the next twelve months over a hundred Frith local history titles will be published! The

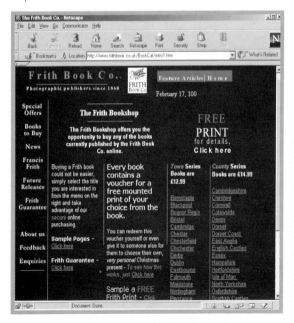

See Frith at www. frithbook.co.uk

day-to-day workings of the archive are very different from how they were in Francis Frith's time: imagine the herculean task of sorting through eleven tons of glass negatives as Frith had to do to locate a particular sequence of pictures! Yet the archive still prides itself on maintaining the same high standards of excellence laid down by Francis Frith, including the painstaking cataloguing and indexing of every view.

It is curious to reflect on how the internet now allows researchers in America and elsewhere greater instant access to the archive than Frith himself ever enjoyed. Many thousands of individual views can be called up on screen within seconds on one of the Frith internet sites, enabling people living continents away to revisit the streets of their ancestral home town, or view places in Britain where they have enjoyed holidays. Many overseas researchers welcome the chance to view special theme selections, such as transport, sports, costume and ancient monuments.

We are certain that Francis Frith would have heartily approved of these modern developments, for he himself was always working at the very limits of Victorian photographic technology.

The Value of the Archive Today

Because of the benefits brought by the computer, Frith's images are increasingly studied by social historians, by researchers into genealogy and ancestory, by architects, town planners, and by teachers and schoolchildren involved in local history projects. In addition, the archive offers every one of

us a unique opportunity to examine the places where we and our families have lived and worked down the years. Immensely successful in Frith's own era, the archive is now, a century and more on, entering a new phase of popularity.

The Past in Tune with the Future

Historians consider the Francis Frith Collection to be of prime national importance. It is the only archive of its kind remaining in private ownership and has been valued at a million pounds. However, this figure is now rapidly increasing as digital technology enables more and more people around the world to enjoy its benefits.

Francis Frith's archive is now housed in an historic timber barn in the beautiful village of Teffont in Wiltshire. Its founder would not recognize the archive office as it is today. In place of the many thousands of dusty boxes containing glass plate negatives and an all-pervading odour of photographic chemicals, there are now ranks of computer screens. He would be amazed to watch his images travelling round the world at unimaginable speeds through network and internet lines.

The archive's future is both bright and exciting. Francis Frith, with his unshakeable belief in making photographs available to the greatest number of people, would undoubtedly approve of what is being done today with his lifetime's work. His photographs, depicting our shared past, are now bringing pleasure and enlightenment to millions around the world a century and more after his death.

AROUND SOUTHAMPTON
An Introduction

SOUTHAMPTON AND HAMPSHIRE'S strongly defended coastline are an intrinsic part of Britain's history. Acting as a symbolic gateway to the world, Southampton Water is the wide estuary of two great rivers - the Test and the Itchen. In the golden days of ocean-going travel, this internationally famous waterway provided first-time visitors to these shores with one of the first glimpses of English soil. Today, the waterfront is more heavily industrialised and the great passenger liners are certainly fewer. But the sense of maritime history is still tangible as one recalls the names of the great liners which once plied these historic waters - the 'Mauretania', the 'Aquitania', the 'Queen Mary' and the 'Queen Elizabeth' among them. The 'Titanic' sailed from Southampton in 1912, and the 'Great Eastern' was moored in Southampton Water prior to her maiden voyage in 1861. Southampton Water has also played a key role in the development of flying boats and sea-planes, which is superbly illustrated in the city's Hall of Aviation. Today, the scene is still a bustling one: you do not have to wait long before you spot an oil tanker, a tug or a ferry, and the low roar of the hydrofoil may arouse your interest as it zips in and out of Southampton Docks. There is always something worth seeing on Southampton Water. But what of the city?

Think of Southampton and we tend to think of passenger liners, freight traffic and ferries. For 500 years it was one of England's leading ports, synonymous with shipbuilding and cruise liners. However, take a stroll through Southampton today and you will see that it is a fascinating mix of ancient and modern. This is a city that has much more to offer than its sprawling docks and bustling waterfront.

An obvious stop on any tour of Southampton has to be the Hall of Aviation. This entertaining attraction is a fitting memorial to the achievements of R J Mitchell, who designed the famous Spitfire fighter aircraft. Here, visitors can climb up to the flight deck of the legendary Sandringham flying boat around which the hall was built. The inside of the flying boat is reminiscent of a first class railway carriage, a classic reminder of the great days of luxury travel. Southampton Water was where these wonderful flying machines used to take off and land; it was a centre for early experimental flying and later a base for long-distance flights.

Not far from the Hall of Aviation is a stark reminder of the 'Titanic'. The old Terminus station, which was opened in 1840 and is still regarded as a wonderful example of classic railway architecture, is where passengers bound for the doomed ship arrived, spending the night at the majestic South Western Hotel prior to her departure the following

ROYAL PIER PAVILION 1908 60415

day. A small quayside memorial marks the spot where the 'Titanic' was berthed prior to her ill-fated maiden voyage in April 1912.

Further along the quay we can begin to trace the old town wall, which dates back to about 1350. This is the start of a walk into history, taking us round the medieval town of Hampton, as Southampton used to be known, and visiting many interesting buildings and landmarks en route. Begin by having a look at the 15th-century God's House Tower, originally the south-east gate of the old town and one of the earliest artillery fortifications in Europe. Heading north brings us to the ruined church of Holy Rood, erected in 1320 and damaged by enemy bombing on the night of 13 November 1940. Known

for centuries as the 'church of the sailors', its ruins have been preserved by the people of the city as a memorial and garden of rest dedicated to those who served in the Merchant Navy and lost their lives at sea. There is also a memorial to the stewards, sailors and firemen who perished in the 'Titanic' disaster.

Our next objective is Bargate, one of the finest medieval gateways in the country, dating back to the late 12th century. A pleasant stroll through the city parks brings us to the statue of Richard Andrews, a 19th-century coach-builder who was five times mayor of Southampton. The statue was unveiled in 1860, a year after his death. This corner of the city is littered with grand monuments.

BARGATE 1908 60428

WESTGATE 1908 60431

The 'Titanic' memorial recalls the engineer-officers who 'showed their high conception of duty and heroism by remaining at their posts', and nearby is Southampton's awesome cenotaph, designed by Edwin Lutyens. Close by is an imposing monument to Issac Watts, the famous hymn-writer, who was a native of the city.

Heading south again, back towards the quay, brings us to Portland Terrace, its elegant Regency design and wrought-iron balconies recalling Southampton's days as a fashionable spa town and resort. Our tour concludes with a return to the old town walls. Soon we reach Arundel Tower and Catchcold Tower, upon which there was an anti-aircraft gun during the Second World War. Shortly we reach the remains of the old castle and the site of the earliest fortifications for the ancient port. Evidence suggests that there may have been a quay here, in the days when seawater reached this far inland. Castle Water Gate, as it is known, may well have had wooden, detachable steps running down to the water's edge.

Beyond Castle Water Gate, we come to Pilgrims Gate, where we leave the old wall and make for the Tudor House overlooking St Michael's Square. This striking timber-framed building dates back to about 1500 and includes some fascinating photographs of Southampton in previous years. Make time to have a look at the Tudor garden which occupies a delightful hidden corner of the city. From here our route takes us south along Bugle Street to Westgate. Henry V marched his army through here on its way to Agincourt. Adjacent to Westgate is the Tudor Merchant Hall, which was moved from St Michael's Square to its present site in 1634.

From here we make for the waterfront and the Wool House, now a maritime museum, which explains in fascinating detail Southampton's role as one of the world's great ports. Nearby is the Mayflower memorial, which commemorates the sailing of the Pilgrim Fathers in 1620, and across the road is the crumbling Royal Pier, damaged by fire in the 1980s.

Francis Frith's photographs of Southampton offer a fascinating glimpse into the changing face of a city. Changes in fashion, shopping and public transport are all represented here, with Frith's images serving as a permanent record of the times. Outside Southampton his photographs of villages and country towns also serve as a reminder of how life used to be. Many of these communities have expanded and evolved almost beyond recognition over the years, while others have stayed largely the same, retaining their distinctive character and identity. The centre of Botley, for example, looks much the same today as it did in the 1950s and '60s when Frith first photographed it. Bursledon and Hamble, on the shores of Southampton Water, are equally timeless in their look and appeal.

Use this book to compare a way of life that many of us still fondly remember with the reality of the present day, examining the numerous changes in urban and rural life, the cars, the buildings, the way we looked and the way we were. These fascinating pictures tell us more about ourselves than we might think. Our memories serve us well, but time and distance lend a certain enchantment that can distort the truth. Francis Frith's photographs, offering a unique social record of the past, can never lie.

BOTLEY, THE MARKET HALL c1955 B544027

HIGH STREET 1908 60418
Many of the buildings in Southampton's famous High Street were destroyed during the Second World War, more than 30 years after this photograph was taken. Horse- drawn trams were introduced to the city in 1879 and electrified in 1900. The tram on the right carries an advert for Brasso. On the left is a large sign for Liptons, the well-known family grocer.

HIGH STREET 1908 60420

Note the tram lines running down the middle of the street. On the left is the imposing Georgian church of All Saints, built in 1795. Badly damaged during World War Two, it was finally demolished in the 1950s. Jane Austen knew this church and its minister, the Reverend Richard Mant. Ahead is the spire of St Lawrence's Church, which was pulled down in 1929 after it became redundant.

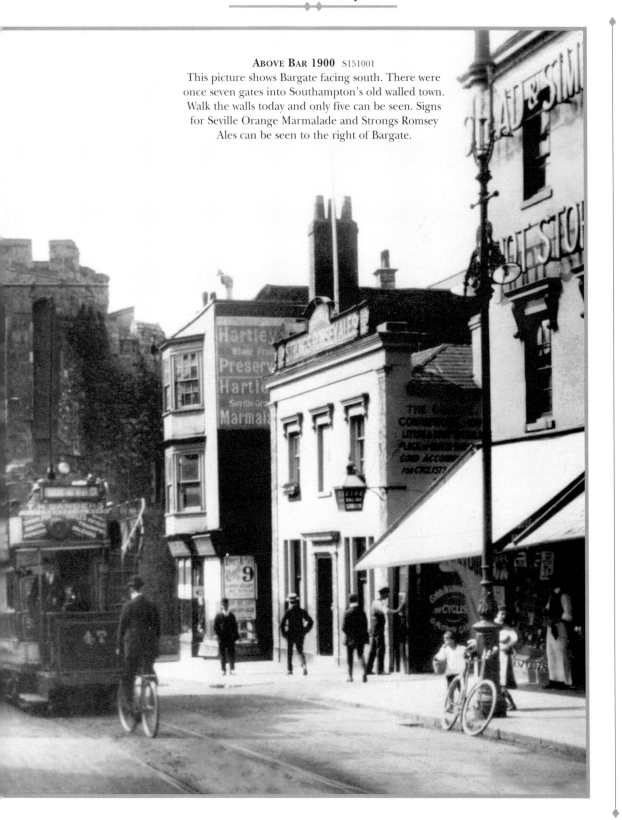

ABOVE BAR 1900 S151001
This picture shows Bargate facing south. There were once seven gates into Southampton's old walled town. Walk the walls today and only five can be seen. Signs for Seville Orange Marmalade and Strongs Romsey Ales can be seen to the right of Bargate.

BARGATE 1908 60428

This early 20th-century photograph shows Bargate at its best. Characterised by pointed arches and fine stonework, the old gate is also renowned for its statue of George III gazing down the High Street, dressed as a Roman and wearing a toga. The fashions, particularly the hats worn by both adults and children, give a strong hint of the Edwardian period.

BARGATE 1908 60426

Up until the 1930s, specially designed trams with dome-shaped tops to fit the arch travelled through Bargate. The adjoining walls and buildings were subsequently destroyed so that traffic bypassed the gate. Rounded flanking towers can be seen in the photograph, and two lions stand either side of the pointed arch.

BARGATE 1908 60427
Slightly reminiscent of a triumphal arch and a famous landmark in Southampton for 800 years or more, Bargate is an appropriate place to begin a walk along what is left of the city walls. The buildings of the High Street can be seen through the central arch.

BARGATE c1955 S151013

BARGATE c1955

By the time this photograph was taken, the buildings either side of Bargate had been demolished to allow traffic to pass freely round each side of it. This medieval building has witnessed the passage of most of the Kings and Queens of England since Henry II.

BARGATE c1955

Bargate was originally built to guard the main road into Southampton. Over the years it has been a toll-gate, prison, guildhall and museum. The original Norman arch dates back to about 1175, and the tower was added a century later. The upper floor used to be the guildhall.

BARGATE c1955 S151009

OLD TOWN WALLS 1892 31336
Southampton's walls and defences were built from stone brought across from the Isle of Wight. This must have been a huge operation, considering that there were one and a quarter miles of walls, seven gates and 29 towers.

OLD TOWN WALLS 1892 31335
Extensive stretches of the old medieval town walls survive today, and many of the towers and gates are still standing. Following the Norman invasion of 1066, Southampton became a key port, and the walls and other buildings are a permanent reminder of Southampton's wealth and prosperity in those days.

WESTGATE 1908 60431

Westgate offers some idea of what it would have been like to live beside the city walls. The portcullis was removed in 1744 when it became 'a nuisance, and of no manner of use'. Henry V and his army marched through Westgate in 1415, on their way to the battle of Agincourt.

WESTGATE 1908

Westgate, dating back to the 14th century, provides access to the south-west corner of the old walled town. One of the finest and best preserved of these remaining fortifications, this was once the main gate to West Quay, which for many centuries was the only quay that could accommodate larger vessels, in the days when seawater reached this far inland.

THE TUDOR HOUSE 1908

The timber-framed Tudor House, one of the city's finest buildings, dates back to about 1500, and has hardly changed at all since this photograph was taken. It became a museum in 1911; many years later, in the early 1980s, its garden was opened to the public as a Tudor garden. Upstairs are aerial photographs of Southampton over the years.

WESTGATE 1908 60430

THE TUDOR HOUSE 1908 60435

THE PILGRIM FATHERS' MONUMENT 1924 76265

THE PILGRIM FATHERS' MONUMENT 1924
This famous monument commemorates the departure of the Pilgrim Fathers to America in August 1620. Travelling aboard the 'Mayflower', the emigrants had to put into Dartmouth and Plymouth following problems with the ship. The memorial was erected opposite the pier on Town Quay in 1913, 11 years before this photograph was taken.

♦

THE PILGRIM FATHERS' MONUMENT 1924
The Pilgrim Fathers' Monument is built of Portland stone and rises 50 feet above the ground. Just visible at the top is a beacon surrounded by Greek pillars and crowned by a copper model of the 'Mayflower' in the form of a weathervane. The ship set sail from nearby West Quay.

THE PILGRIM FATHERS' MONUMENT 1924 76264

GOD'S HOUSE TOWER 1892 31334

On the right of the photograph is the 15th-century God's House Tower, formerly the south-east gate of the old town and one of the earliest artillery fortifications in Europe. A ditch ran alongside the building until the 1850s, which was intended to link Southampton with the Andover Canal and the River Test.

GOD'S HOUSE TOWER 1908 60429

Now Southampton's Archaeological Museum, this used to be the home of the town gunner, with the guns and powder stored here. During the 17th century, when it was the town jail, prisoners of war were held in custody here. The buildings survive as one of the most awe-inspiring defences within the city.

ROYAL PIER PAVILION 1908 60415
The Royal Pier, at the eastern end of Mayflower Park,
was opened in 1833 and for many years was the largest
in the south of England. The pier was reconstructed
during the early 1890s, and the pavilion's distinctive
onion domes were added in the late 1920s. Much of it
was destroyed by fire in 1987.

IN DRY DOCK 1908 60442
Here we see the 'Finland' in Number 6 Dry Dock. The
vessel was not a regular visitor to the port, and could have
been here on charter. Southampton's other main dry
dock, Trafalgar, was opened in 1905 and probably would
have been used by the 'Titanic' had she survived.

THE DOCKS 1917 S151002
The name 'La Plata' was adopted by several ships from 1860 onwards. These vessels sailed to the West Indian islands and South America, carrying passengers and cargo.

THE CIVIC CENTRE c1955 S151046
At the heart of Southampton lies the Civic Centre, with its council offices, law courts and art gallery. The building dates back to the 1930s; soaring above it is the distinctive 182-ft high tower, visible from many parts of the city. Today, Southampton has one of the finest 20th-century British art collections outside London.

THE ANDREWS MONUMENT 1908

This is a remarkably grand and ostentatious monument, even for one of Southampton's most dedicated sons. The statue, the work of eccentric local sculptor Richard Cockle Lucas, bears the inscription: 'As a permanent record of private worth and to honour a career of public usefulness - the fellow townsmen of Richard Andrews, five times mayor of Southampton'.

ON THE COMMON 1908

The Common dates back to medieval times. It was purchased by the town from the manor of Shirley in 1228 for ten silver marks - quite a bargain! Today, no other city in England has such a large area of public common, and within its boundaries more than 350 species of flowering plants and over 100 species of birds have been identified. The rambling building at the centre of the photograph is The Cowheards pub.

THE ANDREWS MONUMENT 1908 60452

ON THE COMMON 1908 60447

THE STAG GATES 1908 60443
A rather complex road junction now marks the spot
where these gates once stood. The gates, signifying the
entrance to the Bevois Mount Estate, date back to
1844, but were removed before World War Two. What
eventually became of them is one of the city's
enduring mysteries, though the stonework may have
been used in the building of the parks rockery by
Brunswick Place.

THE FLOATING BRIDGE 1908 60438

Southampton's famous Floating Bridge enabled foot passengers and traffic to cross the Itchen between the city and the south-eastern suburb of Woolston. The steam-powered floating bridge was in service for 141 years, between 1836 and 1977. A high-level road bridge eventually replaced it.

THE FLOATING BRIDGE c1955 W468003
The Floating Bridge was for many the only way to cross the river at this point. This 1950s photograph somehow captures the spirit of that austere period following the war. Women, some in hats and coats, and men, some in suits and other working apparel, converge at the waterside, many of them on their way to or from work. Notice the small sign on the right, advising the public that bathing here on the hard is strictly prohibited.

WOOLSTON, PORTSMOUTH ROAD c1960 W468029

A fascinating picture of a suburban street. On the extreme left is Palmers, with John Bull tyres and cycle lamp batteries on display in the window. A few doors up is the distinctive facade of a small cinema, or 'flea pit' as they were sometimes known. Until comparatively recently every town had at least one cinema, and cities the size of Southampton often had scores of them. On the right is another relic of the old high street - the National Provincial Bank.

NETLEY, THE ABBEY 1908 60468

Founded in 1239 by the monks of Beaulieu Abbey, Netley Abbey occupies a pretty setting amidst the trees. Close by is Southampton Water. The abbey was dissolved in 1536 and later became a private mansion. In the 18th century it passed to a Southampton builder who was killed by falling tracery as he began to demolish the site.

NETLEY, ST EDWARDS CHURCH c1955 N10004
The church of St Edward the Confessor contains a medieval effigy of a crusader monk, which was found in the wall of nearby Netley Castle and probably came from Netley Abbey.

NETLEY, THE CASTLE c1955 N10085
This imposing building is impressively situated on the shores of Southampton Water. The original castle, built by Henry VIII in 1542 as part of his many coastal defences, has all but disappeared, and was replaced by a large Victorian mansion during the 1880s. However, one surviving relic could be the Tudor archway in the main entrance, possibly part of the old fort.

NETLEY, VICTORIA ROAD c1955 N10003

Pevsner described Netley as 'a Victorian period piece'; its streets of neat family villas and rows of renovated terraced cottages overlooking Southampton Water are certainly striking. Drive through the village and before long you reach the entrance to the Royal Victoria Country Park, formerly the site of the old Netley Hospital.

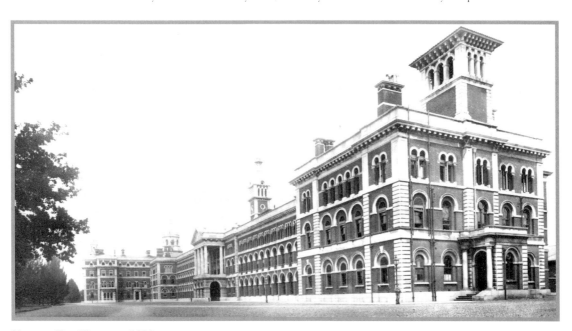

NETLEY, THE HOSPITAL 1908 60465

Today, the chapel, with its distinctive green dome, is all that remains of the old Royal Victoria Military Hospital, opened in 1868 and demolished in 1966. The building was an incredible quarter of a mile long and cost more than £300,000 to construct. The sick, dying and injured were brought here from the war-torn corners of the British Empire; the 570-ft-long pier enabled casualties to be carried ashore from troop ships.

NETLEY, THE ROYAL VICTORIA HOSPITAL c1955 N10014

This must be one of the last photographs of the old military hospital at Netley before most of it disappeared from the shores of Southampton Water in a huge heap of rubble. It was Queen Victoria who originally argued the need for such a hospital; its objective was to care for the gravely-afflicted casualties of war. The building attracted criticism, and a mix-up with the plans resulted in the hospital being built the wrong way round, so that all the wards faced the sunless north.

HAMBLE, THE QUAY c1955 H148023

Famous as a yachting centre, Hamble has long thrived on its close proximity to the river of the same name, with its shipbuilding associations, yacht clubs and marinas. Originally just a small fishing village renowned for oysters, crabs and lobsters, Hamble was later to become a sprawling community with the accent on leisure and the aircraft industry.

HAMBLE
The Village c1955

Despite the steady encroachment of urban and residential development along the shores of Southampton Water, we may be thankful that the quaint little village of Hamble remains intact. Its popularity with visitors ensures that its beauty is preserved and protected for future generations.

◆

HAMBLE
The Village c1955

Pevsner likened Hamble to a West Country fishing village, and he was right to make the comparison. With its steep, winding streets and pretty cottages, there is a definite hint of Devon or Cornwall about it. Take a stroll through the village and you will be surprised at just how many pubs there are. The Victory Inn can be seen down the street, and round the corner, not visible in this picture, is The Bugle, Hamble's famous riverside inn, which probably dates from the 12th century.

HAMBLE, THE VILLAGE c1955 H148123

HAMBLE, THE VILLAGE c1955 H148035

BURSLEDON
The Bridge c1955 B304008
Between the 14th and early 19th centuries, Bursledon
was an important centre for naval shipbuilding, with
the wooded slopes of the River Hamble providing
much of the timber. HMS 'Elephant', Nelson's 74-gun
flagship at the Battle of Copenhagen, was built here by
George Parsons and launched at his yard in 1786.

BURSLEDON, HAMBLE RIVER c1955 B304020

Until the beginning of the 19th century the only crossing of the Hamble was by ferry. The first structure was a toll bridge; today the river is spanned by various busy roads and a motorway - a far cry from the days centuries ago when this river and many others like it on the south coast were coveted by invaders.

BURSLEDON, THE VILLAGE c1960 B304003

Bursledon village consists of two distinct halves - the new and the old. The older part is more interesting and certainly more picturesque, with its streets of quaint old buildings clinging to the banks of the Hamble. Visitors to Bursledon often recall the little Gothic belfry at the entrance to the Roman Catholic Chapel of Our Lady of the Rosary.

OLD BURSLEDON, THE CHURCH c1965 0112043

The church stands halfway up a hill overlooking the village rooftops and contains a large and impressive Norman font. The chancel arch is 13th-century, and the church contains several memorials to former shipbuilders, including Philemon Ewer, who died in 1750. Ewer built seven large ships of war for his majesty's service during the wars with France and Spain.

CADNAM, THE SIR WALTER TYRRELL c1960 C3019

This well-known inn is situated in a peaceful corner of the New Forest, close to Cadnam. Originally the pub was sited nearby and was known as the Stump, named after the one-legged landlady who ran it. It became the Sir Walter Tyrrell in 1929, but was destroyed by fire after the Second World War. It was later rebuilt. Sir Walter Tyrrell was a nobleman at the court of King William Rufus.

CADNAM, THE GREEN C1960 C3024

Not very far from this spot lies the Rufus Stone, which marks the spot where King William Rufus, son of William the Conqueror, was accidentally killed by an arrow shot by Sir Walter Tyrrell while out hunting in nearby Canterton Glen in the summer of 1100. He had supposedly meant to kill a stag, but the arrow glanced and struck Rufus, the most hated of kings.

MARCHWOOD, THE VILLAGE C1965 M315009

A charming village scene that has scarcely changed at all in over 30 years. The old war-time nissen hut, at one time such a familiar sight in the British countryside, has gone, replaced by a car park and children's playground, and the thatched cottages have been renovated and re-thatched.

MARCHWOOD
Magazine Lane c1965

These redbrick cottages have defied the march of time and today look much as they did in the mid 1960s. Even the street lamp is still there. The cottages may look the same, but the surrounding landscape has changed virtually beyond recognition. Modern housing and industrial development crowd in from all directions, making it almost impossible to stand here and spot passing liners on Southampton Water.

◆

ELING
The Quay c1955

Stand on the toll bridge by Eling Tide Mill, where this photograph was taken, and you will see that the tall chimney on the left has gone, as have many of the other industrial units seen in this photograph. Modern storage and container units have taken their place as the emphasis switches from industry to warehousing and unloaded cargo.

MARCHWOOD, MAGAZINE LANE c1965   M315004

ELING, THE QUAY c1955   T243006

ELING
The Quay c1955 T243007

This photograph somehow conveys the feel of a picturesque West Country creek, with its thickly wooded shore and little boats stranded at low tide. The scene has changed little today. Nearby is Eling Tide Mill, the only surviving tide mill in the world still producing flour on a daily basis. Founded over 900 years ago, the site was restored and reopened in 1980 as a working mill and museum.

ELING, ST MARY'S CHURCH C1955 T243004
A short stroll from the toll bridge brings you to the little church of St Mary's. Above the altar hangs an impressive picture of the Last Supper. The chancel arch is a striking feature of the church, as is the 15th-century tower. Much has changed in this area of Hampshire, but little Eling, at the head of Southampton Water, is one tiny corner of the county that seems delightfully timeless.

TOTTON, THE BY-PASS C1965 T243010
Totton, Eling's larger neighbour, once claimed the title of the 'largest village in Hampshire' - though it has expanded so much in recent years that by no stretch of the imagination could it still be described as a village. The old redundant 17th-century bridge over the Test now lies on the north side of the main road.

CALSHOT, THE BEACH c1960 C572001

Calshot has long been popular with local people and holidaymakers for the views it affords of Southampton Water. This stretch of the Hampshire coastline is the perfect spot to watch all the comings and goings on the water. This was the place to come to see the 'Queen Elizabeth' and the 'Queen Mary' - among other great liners from the great days of ocean-going travel.

BOTLEY, THE STATION c1960 B544059

By the Victorian drinking fountain at the entrance to Botley station lies a memorial tablet which reads: 'this stone is erected to perpetuate a most cruel murder committed on the body of Thomas Webb, a poor inhabitant of Swanmore, on 11th February 1800 by John Diggins, a private soldier in the Talbot Fencibles, whose remains are gibbeted on the adjoining common'.

BOTLEY
The Hambledon Hounds c1960 B544301
The hunt assembles at the front of the Bugle pub, a former coaching inn. Note the sturdy porch, similar to that of its opposite neighbour, the Dolphin Hotel. Botley, once a small inland port, stands at the head of navigation on the River Hamble. Barges travelled upstream for corn, coal and timber until the early 20th century.

BOTLEY, THE MARKET HALL c1955 B544027

This photograph shows the Dolphin Hotel on the right of the square, next to the mid-19th century Market Hall. In the days when Botley was an important staging post on the coach route, the village boasted as many as fourteen inns.

BOTLEY, THE CHURCH c1955 B544001

Situated at the western end of the main street, All Saints Church has dormer windows with carved bargeboards and a diamond-shaped clock with a gilded crown. The clock comes from the stables of the 19th-century farmer and journalist William Cobbett, who lived at Fairthorn Farm and described Botley as 'the most delightful village in the world'.

BOTLEY, THE CHURCH 1960 B544040
Stand in the corner of the churchyard and you can see that this view of All Saints Church has hardly changed at all since this photograph was taken. The yew trees are thicker now, and there is a modern extension at the far end of the churchyard.

BOTLEY, SOUTHAMPTON ROAD c1955 B544024
Historian Arthur Mee described Botley as 'a delightful old town with quaint shops, handsome houses, and pretty inns'. William Cobbett was equally fulsome, maintaining that Botley had everything in it that he loved and nothing that he hated. However, he fell out with the local clergyman, declaring that he wanted to horsewhip him in the pulpit for talking such nonsense.

BOTLEY

High Street c1960 B544035

The clock on Botley's Market Hall is still a familiar landmark in the High Street. Just this side of it can be seen the premises of Botley Garages, now a sports shop and a hairdresser's. The swinging AA sign has gone, replaced by one for the sports unit. Small garages like this one were once a familiar sight in Britain's country towns and villages.

BOTLEY, HIGH STREET c1960 B544045

If you compare this photograph with the reality of the scene today, it would seem at first glance as if time has stood still here. However, look a little closer and you can pick out a few subtle changes. The white cottage on the right of the High Street is now the premises of an estate agent, and the ivy which covers the house on the left has gone. However, the portico and the telegraph pole remain. The white fencing on the right has disappeared and iron railings have been added. Typically, the Lloyds Bank branch has gone.

BOTLEY, THE SQUARE c1955 B544021

Elcock's, the little newsagent and tobacconist almost hidden behind a forest of newspaper signs and placards, has been replaced by a beauty therapist, and most of the shops either side of the Bugle Inn have also gone.

BOTLEY, THE BUGLE INN c1960 B544065

The bugler depicted in the pub sign has been replaced, and the old familiar shutters at the windows have gone. When this photograph was taken, this was a Strong's pub. However, the Romsey-based brewery, which was leased to Thomas Strong in 1858, was acquired by Whitbread in 1969 and brewing finally ceased in 1981.

BOTLEY, THE SQUARE c1960 B544053

On the extreme left is Botley Post Office, and next to it is a chemists; the former is now a dress shop, and the latter remains a pharmacy. The Dolphin, managed by Watneys when this photograph was taken, is now a Morland pub. Visit the Dolphin today and you can see that the clock face next to it is now an eye-catching black and gold.

BOTLEY

The Square c1955 B544002

The splendid Market Hall has been home to two artefacts from the distant and recent past. One is a carved block of timber about three feet high, part of a Danish war galley found in the river during the 19th century; the other is a huge china jug adorned with ships and pictures, said to have been the punch jug used at the Farmers Club dinners in the days when Botley was a prosperous market town.

BOTLEY, THE SQUARE c1960 B544044

Here we see the sturdy porticoed front of Botley's famous Market Hall, built in 1848. The turret and clock above were erected by local parishioners to commemorate Queen Victoria's Diamond Jubilee in 1897. Opposite is the premises of W H Lewry, the High Street butcher, which remained in the family until 1999.

BOTLEY, CHURCH LANE c1955 B544028

Take a stroll down Church Lane and you can see that the scene on the right of this photograph has not changed at all. The little cottage on the left has been replaced by a redbrick house, and there is a modern bungalow just to the right of it. The partly timbered building with the large window and the gable end is still there, and is the premises of the local snooker club.

BOTLEY, WINCHESTER ROAD c1955 B544019

The right-hand side of the street has changed almost beyond recognition over the years. Maffey's has gone, and is now a private house with a portico. All the buildings beyond it have been demolished and replaced with modern development. The left-hand side of Winchester Road remains constant, with the pub and the timber-framed cottage still to be seen.

BOTLEY, MILL HILL c1955 B544005

The elegant Georgian house on the right of the road has been converted to offices. To the right of it is the entrance to Botley Mills, an 18th-century mill complex, which is mentioned in the Domesday Book. Just visible on the left of the picture is the stonework of the bridge which carries this road over the River Hamble.

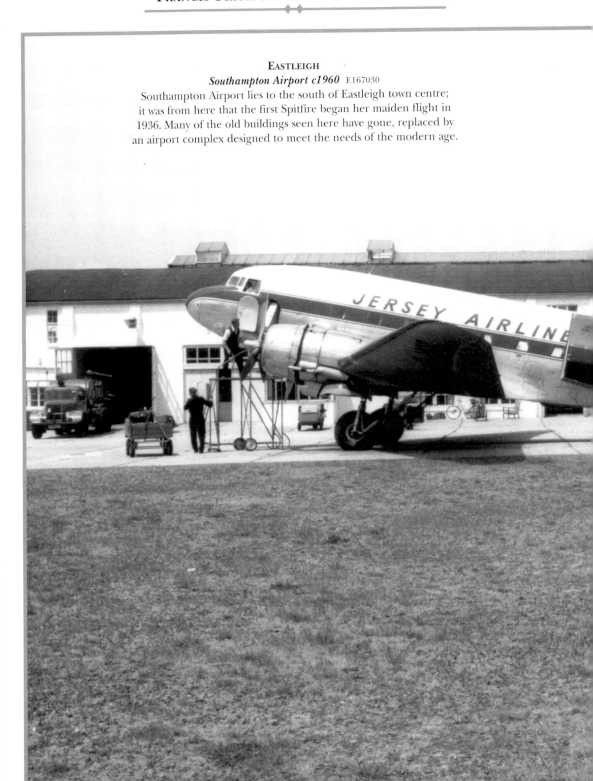

EASTLEIGH
Southampton Airport c1960 E167030
Southampton Airport lies to the south of Eastleigh town centre;
it was from here that the first Spitfire began her maiden flight in
1936. Many of the old buildings seen here have gone, replaced by
an airport complex designed to meet the needs of the modern age.

EASTLEIGH, SOUTHAMPTON AIRPORT C1960 E167032
Hampshire's only commercial airport was once at the centre of a major controversy. Both Southampton and Eastleigh laid claim to its title; the thorny problem was eventually and diplomatically settled by calling it Southampton (Eastleigh) Airport. Passengers and freight are conveyed by regular scheduled airlines to and from all corners of Britain, as well as the Channel Islands and Europe.

EASTLEIGH, SOUTHAMPTON AIRPORT C1960 E167025
The buildings in this photograph look rather dated compared with today's modern airport complexes. The air traffic control centre is housed in a building which rather resembles an old war-time nissen hut; to the right of it is the quaintly-named emergency services rendezvous point.

EASTLEIGH
North Stoneham Church c1960

North Stoneham Church was rebuilt at the end of the 16th century in the Gothic style. One of the more unusual features of this church is the tombstone of 1491 which contains a group of Venetian sailors. These men may have been among the many trading fraternities using Southampton at that time.

EASTLEIGH
Market Street c1955

Originally a village, Eastleigh expanded rapidly around Bishopstoke Junction after the London and South Western Railway Company's carriage works moved here in 1889-90, followed by the locomotive workshops in 1909. Much of the town dates from between 1890 and 1939, and many of its residents were employed by the railway.

EASTLEIGH NORTH STONEHAM CHURCH c1960   E167008

EASTLEIGH, MARKET STREET c1955   E167001

EASTLEIGH
Leigh Road c1960 E167016
What the Army did for Aldershot, the London and South Western
Railway Company did for Eastleigh, helping to transform a
forgotten rural backwater into a bustling and thriving town. The
image of the railway town remains, though many changes have
taken place here in recent years. But Eastleigh is not just about
railways. Many other forms of industry are based here, including
Pirelli Cables and the Mr Kipling bakery.

EASTLEIGH, HIGH STREET c1960 E167020

Ornate lamps and fashionable street furniture have been added to the High Street since this photograph was taken. The trees in the street have been pollarded, and the premises of John Cole and Delbridges have gone. A statue of the 'Railway Man' by sculptor Jill Tweed now stands on this corner, symbolising Eastleigh's link with the railway industry. The statue was unveiled in 1995.

EASTLEIGH, HIGH STREET c1955 E167019

Modern Eastleigh is a grid pattern of late 19th-century and early 20th-century streets, with typical suburban fringes stretching out towards Southampton and Winchester. The geometric criss-crossing roads, the older buildings and the park with its bandstand give the town a separate identity from other towns in the region.

EASTLEIGH, MARKET STREET c1960 E167015

The upper floors of the buildings on the right have hardly changed at all since this photograph was taken. At ground floor level canopied, stylish shop fronts replace the premises of J Baker and Complete House Furnishings. Kingfisher China and Glass replaces Smith Bradbeer & Co on the left. An ornate clock now stands on this busy junction.

EASTLEIGH, MARKET STREET c1965 E167044

This photograph was taken about half-way along Market Street; it shows many shop premises, most of which have changed hands several times in the intervening years. Pricerite is now Peacocks, Lennards is the Abbey National Building Society and Dennis Cox acquired Dewhursts in the early 1990s. The tall, rather distinctive building on the left is now Burtons. The first floor was once a billiards room.

EASTLEIGH, LEIGH ROAD c1960 E167018

This photograph was taken at the front of Eastleigh railway station. The front of the National Provincial Bank, now the National Westminster, has barely changed since 1960. Even the arched entrance on the corner remains the same. The eye-catching Barclays building on the right has made way for modern development, and the adjoining older building with dormer windows now consists of an insurance brokers and a solicitor's office.

EASTLEIGH, LEIGH ROAD c1960 E167002
A fascinating photograph showing Leigh Road at its junction with Market Street. This corner of Eastleigh has changed significantly: the new buildings interposed with the older ones on the left-hand side of the street offer a rich mix of architectural styles. The street is now pedestrianised. The distant building with the steep roof is the Roman Catholic Church of Holy Cross.

EASTLEIGH, THE TOWN HALL c1960 E167022
The old Town Hall is a dignified building of mellow brick with a clock beneath an elegant cupola. The building looks just the same now as it did in about 1960; nowadays, part of it is a dance and arts centre, together with a tourist information centre. Immediately beyond this fine building is The Park, a green lung at the centre of Eastleigh.

EASTLEIGH
Leigh Road c1960 E167012
For so long Eastleigh has been synonymous with marshalling yards and the grime of the railway age. Over the years, the local planners have fought hard to improve the town's image, and in 1977 Eastleigh won a national competition for environmental improvement. Take a stroll through the town and you can see how the town has changed for the better in recent times.

CHANDLERS FORD, WINCHESTER ROAD c1965 C490302
Once a village, Chandlers Ford has now been swallowed up by the suburbs of nearby Southampton and Eastleigh. Chandler was the ancient miller who occupied the little mill in the valley; the ford was negotiated by passing stagecoaches.

Index

Frith Book Co Titles

Frith Book Company publish over a 100 new titles each year. For latest catalogue please contact Frith Book Co.

Town Books 96pp, 100 photos. County and Themed Books 128pp, 150 photos (unless specified) All titles hardback laminated case and jacket except those indicated pb (paperback)

Around Barnstaple	1-85937-084-5	£12.99
Around Blackpool	1-85937-049-7	£12.99
Around Bognor Regis	1-85937-055-1	£12.99
Around Bristol	1-85937-050-0	£12.99
Around Cambridge	1-85937-092-6	£12.99
Cheshire	1-85937-045-4	£14.99
Around Chester	1-85937-090-X	£12.99
Around Chesterfield	1-85937-071-3	£12.99
Around Chichester	1-85937-089-6	£12.99
Cornwall	1-85937-054-3	£14.99
Cotswolds	1-85937-099-3	£14.99
Around Derby	1-85937-046-2	£12.99
Devon	1-85937-052-7	£14.99
Dorset	1-85937-075-6	£14.99
Dorset Coast	1-85937-062-4	£14.99
Around Dublin	1-85937-058-6	£12.99
East Anglia	1-85937-059-4	£14.99
Around Eastbourne	1-85937-061-6	£12.99
English Castles	1-85937-078-0	£14.99
Around Falmouth	1-85937-066-7	£12.99
Hampshire	1-85937-064-0	£14.99
Isle of Man	1-85937-065-9	£14.99
Around Maidstone	1-85937-056-X	£12.99
North Yorkshire	1-85937-048-9	£14.99
Around Nottingham	1-85937-060-8	£12.99
Around Penzance	1-85937-069-1	£12.99
Around Reading	1-85937-087-X	£12.99
Around St Ives	1-85937-068-3	£12.99
Around Salisbury	1-85937-091-8	£12.99
Around Scarborough	1-85937-104-3	£12.99
Scottish Castles	1-85937-077-2	£14.99
Around Sevenoaks and Tonbridge	1-85937-057-8	£12.99

Sheffield and S Yorkshire	1-85937-070-5	£14.99
Shropshire	1-85937-083-7	£14.99
Staffordshire	1-85937-047-0 (96pp)	£12.99
Suffolk	1-85937-074-8	£14.99
Surrey	1-85937-081-0	£14.99
Around Torbay	1-85937-063-2	£12.99
Wiltshire	1-85937-053-5	£14.99
Around Bakewell	1-85937-113-2	£12.99
Around Bournemouth	1-85937-067-5	£12.99
Cambridgeshire	1-85937-086-1	£14.99
Essex	1-85937-082-9	£14.99
Around Great Yarmouth	1-85937-085-3	£12.99
Hertfordshire	1-85937-079-9	£14.99
Isle of Wight	1-85937-114-0	£14.99
Around Lincoln	1-85937-111-6	£12.99
Oxfordshire	1-85937-076-4	£14.99
Around Shrewsbury	1-85937-110-8	£12.99
South Devon Coast	1-85937-107-8	£14.99
Around Stratford upon Avon	1-85937-098-5	£12.99
West Midlands	1-85937-109-4	£14.99

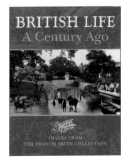

British Life A Century Ago
246 x 189mm
144pp, hardback.
Black and white
Lavishly illustrated with photos from the turn of the century, and with extensive commentary. It offers a unique insight into the social history and heritage of bygone Britain.

1-85937-103-5 £17.99

Available from your local bookshop or from the publisher

Around Bath	1-85937-097-7	£12.99	Mar
County Durham	1-85937-123-x	£14.99	Mar
Cumbria	1-85937-101-9	£14.99	Mar
Down the Thames	1-85937-121-3	£14.99	Mar
Around Exeter	1-85937-126-4	£12.99	Mar
Greater Manchester	1-85937-108-6	£14.99	Mar
Around Guildford	1-85937-117-5	£12.99	Mar
Around Harrogate	1-85937-112-4	£12.99	Mar
Around Leicester	1-85937-073-x	£12.99	Mar
Around Liverpool	1-85937-051-9	£12.99	Mar
Around Newark	1-85937-105-1	£12.99	Mar
Northumberland and Tyne & Wear			
	1-85937-072-1	£14.99	Mar
Around Oxford	1-85937-096-9	£12.99	Mar
Around Plymouth	1-85937-119-1	£12.99	Mar
Around Southport	1-85937-106-x	£12.99	Mar
Welsh Castles	1-85937-120-5	£14.99	Mar
Around Belfast	1-85937-094-2	£12.99	Apr
Canals and Waterways	1-85937-129-9	£17.99	Apr
Down the Severn	1-85937-118-3	£14.99	Apr
East Sussex	1-85937-130-2	£14.99	Apr
Exmoor	1-85937-132-9	£14.99	Apr
Gloucestershire	1-85937-102-7	£14.99	Apr
Around Horsham	1-85937-127-2	£12.99	Apr
Around Ipswich	1-85937-133-7	£12.99	Apr
Ireland (pb)	1-85937-181-7	£9.99	Apr
Kent Living Memories	1-85937-125-6	£14.99	Apr
London (pb)	1-85937-183-3	£9.99	Apr
New Forest	1-85937-128-0	£14.99	Apr
Scotland (pb)	1-85937-182-5	£9.99	Apr
Around Southampton	1-85937-088-8	£12.99	Apr
Stone Circles & Ancient Monuments			
	1-85937-143-4	£17.99	Apr
Sussex (pb)	1-85937-184-1	£9.99	Apr
Colchester (pb)	1-85937-188-4	£8.99	May
County Maps of Britain			
	1-85937-156-6 (192pp)	£19.99	May
Leicestershire (pb)	1-85937-185-x	£9.99	May

Lincolnshire	1-85937-135-3	£14.99	May
Around Newquay	1-85937-140-x	£12.99	May
Nottinghamshire (pb)	1-85937-187-6	£9.99	May
Redhill to Reigate	1-85937-137-x	£12.99	May
Victorian & Edwardian Yorkshire			
	1-85937-154-x	£14.99	May
Around Winchester	1-85937-139-6	£12.99	May
Yorkshire (pb)	1-85937-186-8	£9.99	May
Berkshire (pb)	1-85937-191-4	£9.99	Jun
Brighton (pb)	1-85937-192-2	£8.99	Jun
Dartmoor	1-85937-145-0	£14.99	Jun
East London	1-85937-080-2	£14.99	Jun
Glasgow (pb)	1-85937-190-6	£8.99	Jun
Kent (pb)	1-85937-189-2	£9.99	Jun
Victorian & Edwardian Kent			
	1-85937-149-3	£14.99	Jun
North Devon Coast	1-85937-146-9	£14.99	Jun
Peak District	1-85937-100-0	£14.99	Jun
Around Truro	1-85937-147-7	£12.99	Jun
Victorian & Edwardian Maritime Album			
	1-85937-144-2	£17.99	Jun
West Sussex	1-85937-148-5	£14.99	Jun
Churches of Berkshire	1-85937-170-1	£17.99	Jul
Churches of Dorset	1-85937-172-8	£17.99	Jul
Churches of Hampshire	1-85937-207-4	£17.99	Jul
Churches of Wiltshire	1-85937-171-x	£17.99	Jul
Derbyshire (pb)	1-85937-196-5	£9.99	Jul
Edinburgh (pb)	1-85937-193-0	£8.99	Jul
Herefordshire	1-85937-174-4	£14.99	Jul
Norwich (pb)	1-85937-194-9	£8.99	Jul
Ports and Harbours	1-85937-208-2	£17.99	Jul
Somerset and Avon	1-85937-153-1	£14.99	Jul
South Devon Living Memories			
	1-85937-168-x	£14.99	Jul
Warwickshire (pb)	1-85937-203-1	£9.99	Jul
Worcestershire	1-85937-152-3	£14.99	Jul
Yorkshire Living Memories			
	1-85937-166-3	£14.99	Jul

FRITH PRODUCTS & SERVICES

Francis Frith would doubtless be pleased to know that the pioneering publishing venture he started in 1860 still continues today. More than a hundred and thirty years later, The Francis Frith Collection continues in the same innovative tradition and is now one of the foremost publishers of vintage photographs in the world. Some of the current activities include:

Interior Decoration

Today Frith's photographs can be seen framed and as giant wall murals in thousands of pubs, restaurants, hotels, banks, retail stores and other public buildings throughout the country. In every case they enhance the unique local atmosphere of the places they depict and provide reminders of gentler days in an increasingly busy and frenetic world.

Product Promotions

Frith products have been used by many major companies to promote the sales of their own products or to reinforce their own history and heritage. Brands include Hovis bread, Courage beers, Scots Porage Oats, Colman's mustard, Cadbury's foods, Mellow Birds coffee, Dunhill pipe tobacco, Guinness, and Bulmer's Cider.

Genealogy and Family History

As the interest in family history and roots grows world-wide, more and more people are turning to Frith's photographs of Great Britain for images of the towns, villages and streets where their ancestors lived; and, of course, photographs of the churches and chapels where their ancestors were christened, married and buried are an essential part of every genealogy tree and family album.

A series of easy-to-use CD Roms is planned for publication, and an increasing number of Frith photographs will be able to be viewed on specialist genealogy sites. A growing range of Frith books will be available on CD.

The Internet

Already thousands of Frith photographs can be viewed and purchased on the internet. By the end of the year 2000 some 60,000 Frith photographs will be available on the internet. The number of sites is constantly expanding, each focussing on different products and services from the Collection.

Some of the sites are listed below.

www.townpages.co.uk
www.icollector.com
www.barclaysquare.co.uk
www.cornwall-online.co.uk

For background information on the Collection look at the three following sites:

www.francisfrith.com
www.francisfrith.co.uk
www.frithbook.co.uk

Frith Products

All Frith photographs are available Framed or just as Mounted Prints, and can be ordered from the address below. From time to time other products - Address Books, Calendars, Table Mats, etc - are available.

For further information:
if you would like further information on any of the above aspects of the Frith business please contact us at the address below:
**The Francis Frith Collection,
Frith's Barn, Teffont, Salisbury, Wiltshire,
England SP3 5QP.**
Tel: +44 (0)1722 716 376 Fax: +44 (0)1722 716 881   Email: uksales@francisfrith.com

---

To receive your FREE Mounted Print

Mounted Print
Overall size 14 x 11 inches

Cut out this Voucher and return it with your remittance for £1.50 to cover postage and handling. Choose any photograph included in this book. Your SEPIA print will be A4 in size, and mounted in a cream mount with burgundy rule lines, overall size 14 x 11 inches.

Order additional Mounted Prints at HALF PRICE (only £7.49 each*)

If there are further pictures you would like to order, possibly as gifts for friends and family, acquire them at half price (no additional postage and handling required).

Have your Mounted Prints framed*

For an additional £14.95 per print you can have your chosen Mounted Print framed in an elegant polished wood and gilt moulding, overall size 16 x 13 inches (no additional postage and handling required).

> *** IMPORTANT!**
> These special prices are only available if ordered using the original voucher on this page (no copies permitted) and at the same time as your free Mounted Print, for delivery to the same address

Frith Collectors' Guild

From time to time we publish a magazine of news and stories about Frith photographs and further special offers of Frith products. If you would like 12 months FREE membership, please return this form.

Send completed forms to:
The Francis Frith Collection, Frith's Barn, Teffont, Salisbury, Wiltshire SP3 5QP

for FREE and Reduced Price Frith Prints

Picture no.	Page number	Qty	Mounted @ £7.49	Framed + £14.95	Total Cost
		1	**Free of charge***	£	£
			£7.49	£	£
			£7.49	£	£
			£7.49	£	£
			£7.49	£	£
			£7.49	£	£

* Post & handling	£1.50

Book Title . . . . **Total Order Cost** £

Please do not photocopy this voucher. Only the original is valid, so please cut it out and return it to us.

I enclose a cheque / postal order for £ . . . .
made payable to 'The Francis Frith Collection'
OR please debit my Mastercard / Visa / Switch / Amex card

Number . . . .

Expires . . . . Signature . . . .

Name Mr/Mrs/Ms . . . .

Address . . . .

. . . .

. . . .

. . . . Postcode . . . .

Daytime Tel No . . . .   Valid to 31/12/01

The Francis Frith Collectors' Guild

Please enrol me as a member for 12 months free of charge.

Name Mr/Mrs/Ms . . . .

Address . . . .

. . . .

. . . .

. . . . Postcode . . . .